Introduction

I need no introduction; my name is on the cover. If by some reason you don't have it, it's Thane Pullan. This book is about my experiences of having a disability, how society can improve treatment of people with disabilities and my own psychological theories, even though I have no training in psychology whatsoever.

A part of me regrets not taking advantage of state education. I have considered getting additional formal qualifications. However, it would be utter lunacy to spend thousands of dollars and a few years of my life just so I have a bit of paper that I have no practical use for, because I am self-employed. Aside from the fact that the education system is entirely flawed due to standardised testing, there is a wonderful thing called the internet, which has all the facts you could ever want. I have used the internet to learn programming, and also psychology very recently. This will come out in the disability attraction chapter, although some of my knowledge is taken from books. To be clear, I don't believe people should do what I did. You should absolutely take advantage of cheap state education while you can. Otherwise, you'll be stuck in low-wage jobs in most cases. Do as I say, not as I do.

I consider myself a very honest person. It is not in my nature to sugar-coat things or hold back. My brother has a theory that since I can't speak, it takes a long time for me to get anything out. So I have a habit of just communicating my immediate thoughts. I have never learned tact, and generally don't think before I speak, especially in live conversations. I value honesty, but find it's rare among people. I also find that when people say they want honesty, but if it is directed towards them they actually don't. Personally, though, I prefer people to be honest and direct with me. That makes it easier to deal with them. I have since learned that some people use the appearance of honesty as a deception tactic, so I am mindful of that. My writing will reflect my honesty. However, there are some aspects of my life I won't go into. few things that will help me, and also other people. It is human nature to care about issues only affecting ourselves. This is true for me to an extent, but I regularly speak out on issues that have nothing to do with me. I try to be knowledgeable about many different issues and be diverse with my commentary. It's good to expand your mind. I never used to pay much attention to disability issues but would comment on them occasionally. I have since become more involved in the area of disabilities, particularly when I realised there was work to be done. It's a strong interest but I also have many other strong interests, too. These include but are not limited to income inequality, racism, homophobia, sustainable economics and climate change.

I am also big on changing people's attitudes and the way people think. I do this quite a bit on blogs. I have had people comment, saying my blogs help them see people with disabilities differently. This was never my intention, but it is certainly a good unintended consequence. It gives me encouragement to keep doing what I am doing. I understand people have their own reasons for thinking the way they do. I will address this as well as examining the thought processes of people with disabilities. I hope this book is helpful for both sides.

I used to be far more capitalistic but have moved towards doing things out of passion like stand-up comedy and now book writing. From a very early age I was selling things. My business ambitions continued when I left school. Recently I have realised that happiness, not money, makes you successful. I still aspire to get a certain level of wealth; it makes it easier to get hot gold diggers. I am moving a bit towards doing things that I enjoy to make money, but will still maintain my business interests. I think if I could be a comedian and inform people through books, these things could be fulfilling. My view is that if you can comfortably live and stop your ambitions there, you're generally happier than most. The research backs this up. I do want a bit more but I also want to educate and entertain people. I have found ways of doing this, so I would say I am pretty happy with the direction of my life.

Many people consider me an upbeat person. For years, I couldn't imagine why. I very frequently swear on blogs and constantly complain. I thoroughly enjoy this style of writing. I like constantly swearing in a humorous fashion. This entertains me. I was searching for disability quotes and some of the stuff I found was utterly depressing. I have now come to the conclusion that people consider me upbeat because I just laugh and make fun of my experiences. I make people laugh. When I am not making people laugh, I try to be informative. This is different from some other people who just whine without any humour or underlying point. I think that this is why my style seems upbeat. To me, I just complain a lot and just make jokes because that's the kind of person I am. I used to find it annoying when people considered me upbeat and positive; now I consider this a good thing. The style in this book will be mostly informative. I hope you enjoy it.

Patronizing

Let me start off with a topic very easy for me to speak about and poke fun at: patronizers. I have changed my attitude towards patronizers. I have realised that they have their reasons for acting the way they do: specifically, ignorance caused by the lack of visibility of people with disabilities. People deal best with what they know. If they haven't interacted with people with disabilities, this could lead to them being uncomfortable or ignorant about how to treat them. However, this doesn't make people who patronize any less annoying. I mainly poke fun at them just because I find it entertaining.

If you're offended by the following two sections because you don't want to be told how to behave, I really couldn't care less. I don't want to be patted on the head, among other things. Frankly, my desire not to be patted on the head outweighs any discomfort you may have from reading this. It is not my desire to lecture. This book is about education and examining where such behaviour is coming from.

There are several types of patronizers. The first is people who speak slowly and loudly to you, as if you are sitting on a giant hearing aid, as I say in my stand-up. This must require an extra layer of thought process, whether conscious or unconscious. If you're treating people with disabilities differently, on some level you must think about how you should treat them. An interviewer once told me he had to fight the urge to speak slowly and loudly. He said it was similar to talking to a foreigner who doesn't understand much English. I have always thought patronizing behaviour was conscious. One looks at a person with a disability and makes a conscious decision to treat him differently. However, the conversation that I had opens up the possibility of this behaviour being unconscious for some. I also note that you can tell some people to stop doing what they are doing, but they will completely ignore you, particularly when they are drunk. In this situation I tend just to laugh.

There are also people who call me a boy despite my being nearly 29. Though perhaps my young-looking face contributes somewhat. This behaviour is also probably unconscious for the most part. I feel that while it is more subtle, it can be the most demeaning, along with being patted on the head. The head-patting is easier to poke fun at, so it doesn't bother me as much. I say I want to bark at them.

Then there are people who say, "It's good to see you out and about" and that you're an inspiration. Let's take the first. This annoys me. The mere appearance of a person with a disability shouldn't excite anyone. We're just people living our lives. Our going out should be normal, not special. If they just left it at "It's good to see you" then I wouldn't mind. It's just something about "out and about" that sounds extra patronizing. So the first tip of this book is to just leave it at "It's good to see you". This personalises things. You may get a better reception.

I also used to find it very annoying when people find me inspirational, especially when I am doing normal things. I have, however, come to the conclusion that if I bring joy to people's lives that's not a bad thing. However, please avoid calling people with disabilities inspirational unless they actually do something that is inspirational. Or, alternatively, feel free to keep quiet about it. Some people who have a disability feel that they're being objectified: that you're using them for inspiration rather than seeing them as a person. To be clear, I don't subscribe to this assertion myself, though I certainly agree that we are not here to inspire you. Again, on a personal level, I no longer mind being called an "inspiration". This is partly because I know I am inspirational for other things, such as creating my own software so I can perform stand-up, for performing stand-up, for saying what I mean, and also for my intelligence and wit.

The thinking behind this "inspirational" idea comes from the misconception that our lives are hard. This is only true to an extent. Let me explain why thinking this way not be as accurate as you think. People have the ability to adapt to circumstances. This is especially true for most people who have disabilities. I know that for me personally, I have known only this life. It is my normality. I don't consider that I have challenges in my life; I consider I have a life. Any extra obstacles become normality and routine and I don't think much about them. Of course, I speak for myself rather than for all people with disabilities. People should not think my life is hard, because it's not. I won't lie; some parts of my life suck, but many parts of many people's lives suck, too. Therefore, I lead a normal life. Some parts of my life are better than most. For members of society who have a disability to be integrated, this attitude needs to go away. While some people who experience disabilities may like this attitude, others may just feel annoyed.

Some people assume you're mentally challenged if you are in a wheelchair. To those people: there's nothing wrong with the way I think. I can't say the same for you. I remember once when I was clubbing once with a friend, a person abused him, saying I couldn't make a decision to drink. I think I screamed, but don't think anyone heard me over the music. I was furious. This person displayed such a level of ignorance. While some people with disabilities are mentally challenged, to assume people with disabilities have low intelligence shows you are ignorant beyond belief. I remember once joining a group in which nobody spoke to me, in part because some didn't know if I could understand. This is ludicrous. Why didn't they just ask me? If you have this assumption, it might be an idea to attempt to communicate with the person: your assumption has every chance of being wrong. It's not a good feeling to be at a gathering and nobody talks to you. I cannot talk, which contributes as well. I am also a blunt prick. When people don't communicate with someone, it does not make them feel integrated into the situation. They could give up. Giving up does nothing to enlighten and educate people who have such ignorance, so such behaviour in society will continue.

Perhaps the ultimate annoyance I have experienced was a woman crying over me. Literally! I tried to laugh and look away but she said "No" and proceeded to continue occupying my attention. That was by far one of the most uncomfortable moments of my life. I have no idea why she was crying. Perhaps it was pity. Perhaps I reminded her of someone else. Either way, it was a terrible experience and I didn't know what to do. I don't need to say: don't do this, ever!

My friend in a chair got annoyed one day that a person asked if we were having a race when we were riding in the street. This didn't annoy me, but I could see her point of view. I viewed it as the stranger trying to connect with us. Then I thought she should have just commented on the weather instead. It's the equivalent of people saying that I'll get a speeding ticket or telling me to not drink and drive. People think these things are funny. I have heard these things roughly a million times. I joke that these things just are not original.

Also think before you go rushing to help people with disabilities; I would suggest that you ask if they want help first. Some of us like to be as independent as possible. If you automatically give help, you may be taking their power and control away from them. Depending on their situation, they could have very little of such independence. Some will be insulted by your asking. Some could expect you to help automatically. Therefore, there is no good solution to this situation. But if you feel the need to help, I think asking is the better option. Personally, I am not likely to refuse help, though at times I have considered it totally unnecessary and annoying.

There are people who will give you things like balloons or other novelty items for no apparent reason. I find this very patronizing and annoying. If I want something, I will ask. However, if other people are getting the same stuff themselves I see no harm in offering such things to a person with a disability, although some would like to be independent or ask for the items themselves. Some however, would consider you rude if you don't ask. Asking may be the easier option.

You can, however, give me cash or shots without asking. I don't mind that. Give as much as you want.

You get ridiculously stupid questions when you have a disability. I was going through airport security and I was asked if I was going on a plane. I was at a concert and someone asked if I liked music. This could be a combination of people trying to make conversation and not knowing the person's intelligence level. If you ask me a ridiculously stupid question I will make fun of the question later.

Alternative annoying interactions

It's a regular complaint in the disability community that spouses are praised for being with a person with a disability. This is just downright offensive. First, in normal relationships the person sees past the disability. Second, in abnormal relationships they are with him or her because of the disability, for completely cynical reasons. I'll discuss this in a later chapter. Either way, you shouldn't be praising the spouse. It's insulting to the person they're with. This says more about you than the spouse. If you don't think you could date a person with a disability, you're just like eighty percent of people, so I won't fault you too much. However, to me, this comes across as narrow-minded and ignorant. It does not say to me that you think that their relationship is normal. How can it? I would point out that the emotion of love can overcome a disability. Yes, I will admit that spouses would do more in certain situations, but this is also a part of being in love. You may be inevitably annoying the partner, also. This tells them you don't think their partner is normal.

Directing questions to the spouse, instead of the person with a disability, about that person, is a terrible idea. If you want to know something about the person, ask them, especially if they are sitting right there. Doing anything else is incredibly rude. Let the person speak for themselves. I understand that you may be uncomfortable speaking to the person. But the number one way to get over your discomfort is to do the thing you're not comfortable doing, at least in my experience. Resolving your discomfort allows you to be better in such situations in future.

People ask what is wrong with a person. This comes from natural human curiosity. I don't mind this question on a personal level. However, I'd advise against using the term "wrong". Asking why someone is in a wheelchair would be better, in my opinion. Some people would still be annoyed just by your asking. I also ponder what difference it makes to your life. However, I understand that humans are naturally curious. So if you feel the need to ask, just ask: why are they in a wheelchair? etc.

Some people don't like to be asked questions about their disability. I would fall into this category. I know this is incredibly weird considering I am writing a book about disability, and trade off it in my comedy. I don't really mind answering questions, unless they come from strangers online who just randomly found a person with a disability on Facebook, etc. I especially don't like answering questions about sex from strangers on the other side of the world. Some people with disabilities dislike questions about disabilities more than I do. I think that's fair enough. Some people don't mind answering. I think I am pretty mixed on the issue, but generally I don't mind. It rather depends who you are talking to. I suggest just Googling what you want to know unless there are signals indicating otherwise.

"How fast a wheelchair goes" could be considered an annoying question. Aside from normal curiosity, humans have a strange fascination with vehicles. This is something I don't share; maybe it's a combination of being gay and a nerd. Again I don't particularly see the relevance to people's lives but don't really mind answering this question. It is, however, very repetitive. I get asked this a lot. I think it's a way to make conversation.

Also, it's probably a bad idea to say you know what it's like to have a disability because you were on crutches or because you were in a wheelchair for a few weeks. Some people can be really annoyed with this and suggest that the speaker try being incontinent and see if it's the same thing. I am not incontinent and don't really mind the statement. It's probably a way of reaching out, but it's probably not the best way to go.

Reactions are also mixed about people saying a person is "hot" for someone in a wheelchair. My view is that this is questionable language and probably not the best direction to go. I tend to agree with the people who say that if you want to call someone hot, just call them hot, and leave the disability out of it. It also sends the message that people with disabilities are usually ogres.

Some people don't like other people resting their arm on a wheelchair or leaning in some other way. I don't necessarily mind it. However, I find myself getting very annoyed when a stranger does it. My wheelchair is not there for your convenience. However, I would say it depends. I am more likely to let you lean on my chair if you don't push my arm out of the way to do it. That actually happened and it was infuriating. In general, don't do this. It's a personal space issue. Some people feel their wheelchair is a part of them. I don't subscribe to this belief. Asking is always polite. Also, if my movements are restricted one tiny bit because you are resting your arm on my wheelchair, that's not acceptable in my view. Perhaps this is unreasonable, but I don't care.

Do not, under any circumstance, put drinks on a wheelchair's tray. This also applies to other items such as bags, but especially drinks. Trays vibrate because of movements and the drink could go to the edge and fall off. It's a terrible idea, particularly when dancing. I get very annoyed when people do this in nightclubs that have tables around. It means I have to stop dancing until the drink is shifted. Again, it is polite to ask before doing such a thing.

Relationships

Sex education for people with disabilities may be an uncomfortable topic. However, not teaching them about sex can lead to rape if they don't understand what sex is. It is essential, therefore, that this topic is taken seriously. It is clear that abstinence-only education does not work. It only results in more unprotected sex and pregnancy. If you don't teach people how to protect themselves, they won't do it. This is simple logic. I expect the same applies to people who have disabilities. People need to know how to protect themselves, regardless.

This becomes problematic when dealing with people with IQs below the consent threshold. However, the consequences of not teaching people with learning disabilities about sex include a higher rate of pregnancy and sexually transmitted infections. I suggest that people look at the consequences of not teaching them what's not OK and how to respond appropriately. It is extremely reckless, in my opinion, to brush this issue under the carpet.

If people are capable enough to have a sex life, they must be allowed to do so. Denying people the opportunity of having sex will probably alienate them and push them away. We have desires, too. It is ludicrous to deny this if we're intelligent enough to maintain a sex life. I was lucky; I got offered a female prostitute when I was 21. I did not go through with it. I was gay and was really confused at that time. Two or three years later I came out of the closet. My parents accepted things and let a guy move in at one stage. I consider my parents progressive on this issue. You just have to allow people to live their lives.

I came out when I was 23 or 24. Being gay and in a wheelchair was extremely problematic since it was not as if I could go out or have guys over. Luckily, though, I didn't really have the desire to do this. It took me a fair while to realise I was gay. After that I tried to tell my parents multiple times, but couldn't. I would always freeze. Part of the reason was that my family was somewhat religious and Christianity taught that being gay was a sin. This contributed heavily to my fears. One day I simply spelt out the word "gay" and tried to get out of the room as fast as possible. To my surprise, they were completely cool with it. I now believe it was ludicrous for me not to come out sooner because of religious reasons. But what's done is done.

I never considered myself hot. When someone wanted to view me on a webcam it was certainly a nice experience. Nobody had really had found me attractive before. However, later I got on a dating site and guys were calling me hot all the time. So I changed my mind about my physical attractiveness. I know that I am hot. However, being hot simply doesn't help in getting sex with desirable guys when you're in a wheelchair and cannot speak. Unfortunately, I compare it to being 70 in your 20s. It certainly feels unfair. Many people with disabilities don't consider themselves hot and I understand why.

According to a survey, eighty percent of people would not consider a relationship with a person with a disability. I expect that the casual sex figure is lower, but not by much. A guy said he wasn't keen because I couldn't respond. To my surprise one guy, whose sister has a disability, outright refused me and cited this as the reason. You'd think someone like him would be more open-minded, not less. Most people are simply not comfortable with the idea of sex with anybody who is different from them. People think that because we have disabilities, we are fragile and asexual. I am wondering if society changed so people with disabilities were viewed more equally it would bring the unwillingness percentage down.

While such a high percentage of people won't have sex with a person with a disability, many turn to hiring prostitutes. Some people frown on this. These people should mind their own business and stop inflicting their beliefs on others. Prostitution is a private contract between two adults. It should be legal and regulated. If prostitution is not legalised, it will still happen. The difference is that the poor will get prosecuted far more often. Sex workers rarely engage in sex work because they enjoy the job, but you can say this for the majority of jobs people do. It is legal in some countries. It is even subsidised for people with disabilities in places like Norway.

Disability sex preferred

There are people that actually prefer sex with a person with a disability; these people are called DPWs (Devotees, Pretenders, Wannabes) or fetishists. The disability community is largely mixed in its reception of these people. When I first heard about them I gathered that most people won't sleep with me anyway. So if these people find me attractive, for whatever reason, that is good by me. However I later learned about the psychological aspects of this attraction. The next section will go into the more abusive side of this. It is important to remember that not everyone who has this attraction is abusive. If I wasn't happily single I would not date a guy with this attraction. I would probably have casual fun if I found a hot guy with this attraction. Though I encountered someone recently who displayed signs of this attraction, I wasn't really keen. But maybe that was because he said he wanted to have a relationship down the track before we even met. This is a bad sign. He appeared to forget about me and I was fine with that.

DPWs are mainly thought of as wanting relationships with people with disabilities. There are a number of theories on why people have this attraction. Most involve events in childhood such as encountering people with disabilities or feeling people with disabilities have special privileges. Pretenders like to pretend they have a disability. Wannabes actually want to acquire a disability; some may harm themselves to acquire it. About half of devotees occasionally pretend and about five percent are Wannabes. Some devotees have been known to follow people with disabilities and also share pictures with other devotees, although I think that this would happen less due to the internet. Some DPWs partner with each other as a compromise. Some may go on disability dating sites or get jobs in the disability sector.

Disability fetishists may come under the DPW spectrum. Some people with disabilities say fetishists objectify them, as they like them for their disability rather than for who they are. I don't really have a problem with this on a personal level. Then again, I only engage in casual relationships nowadays. Through a conversation with a fetishist I concluded that this might be related to the desire to dominate. One also said that he likes people with disabilities because they're weak. This may not be all DPWs or fetishists, but certainly some. People have reported controlling and narcissistic abuse to me. I think it's important not to paint everyone with the same brush. I believe only a percentage of DPWs have power and control issues and only some of that number would go on to abuse their partners. However, the fact that this is not discussed on devotee sites and people with disabilities are given no information about this issue, is of great concern.

Abuse

There is a sinister side to those who go after people with disabilities that is not discussed in the mainstream. Some individuals seek out people with disabilities because they want someone who is easy to control. They are in essence attracted to someone who is vulnerable and weak. They want a glorified pet. These people are more likely to abuse a spouse or partner. I don't mean physical abuse. These people simply want someone to control and they target people with disabilities. If I wasn't happily single, there is no way in hell I'd go on a dating site for people with disabilities.

These people may be narcissists or and/or psychopaths. Both of these types lack empathy. Some abusers manage not to be angry with the person with a disability, ever. This is because some abusers don't want to lose the person they're abusing. Perhaps this is why devotees are not considered threats; the abuse is psychological rather than physical. The victim may be unaware of the abuse.

Narcissists in particular may be attracted to the idea of being thought of as great because they are with a person with a disability.

I have stated before that if a partner never gets angry he or she might be an abuser. Other signs of a narcissist specifically include using pronouns excessively, always blaming others, never showing interest in others apart from a select few, needlessly putting you down, excessively talking you up, and treating children or pets cruelly. Further signs of game-playing include your partner being (or acting) unusually dumb or excessively letting you make decisions. Unfortunately, if you are in a relationship for a significant amount of time, you will probably dismiss these signs. It's best to take note of these signs as early as possible, and stay away if you think you come across a likely abuser.

If your ex is an abuser, cut them out of your life. There is no point in remaining friends with an abuser. If you have custody arrangements etc., it's important that you maintain only the minimum amount of contact and conversation necessary to uphold these agreements, and no more. If your ex was a narcissist, you fell in love with an illusion.

The narcissist has many inner demons and projects an entirely false version of himself or herself out to the world. Narcissists are almost certainly pathological liars. You don't really know them. You see only what they want you to think of them. Once you're out, it's better to stay well away. A narcissist doesn't see people as friends, but mere objects to use when he likes.

The sad fact is that eighty percent of people will not consider a relationship with a person with a disability and people with disabilities are targeted by people who want to abuse them. This obviously makes relationship abuse much more likely for those with disabilities. People with disabilities may be starved for attention and could be easy to charm, similar to intellectuals. Of course I don't advise avoiding relationships altogether. But people with disabilities need to be extra cautious. Avoid dating sites specifically for people with disabilities and devotee sites.

Other forms of abuse

The good news is that people with disabilities are less likely to get assaulted or robbed by a stranger, although they are less likely to report crime, so that may be a factor. Unfortunately, most of the abuse comes from people they know, such as a caregiver. An abuser might form a relationship with a person because he/she has a disability. People with disabilities are about twice as likely to get assaulted. Women are much more likely to get sexually assaulted, particularly if they live in a care home or have an intellectual disability. It can occur more than once by the same person. Sometimes it will happen over and over. Children with disabilities also have a much higher likelihood of being abused in some way.

This is possibly because the report rate is much lower than for abuse to other people. Caregivers can inflict abuse. If the person with the disability has limited options or lives in a care home, he could be hesitant to report the abuse. The person also may lack the mental capacity to report or understand the abuse if they have an intellectual disability, so it is vital that everybody understand the various forms of abuse. Neglect is also a form of abuse and is probably more common among caregivers. If someone acts fearful of a caregiver or avoids eye contact, it's possible that they are being abused. In addition, sudden behavioural changes in people with learning disabilities could indicate abuse, particularly if they act differently around a specific person.

The criminal justice system may have problems with accommodating the needs of people with disabilities, particularly those with communication or intellectual impairments. This could be one of the reasons why arrest rates are so low. I expect this is a bigger problem in small towns. Hiring a person with the necessary skills to communicate with people who have impairments is a good idea. Such a person could travel between towns. Making sure people have options and are not stuck in their living situations could also help prevent or stop abuse.

Other forms of abuse include financial. People with disabilities may be grateful for friendship and could be more likely to give things away or make sacrifices. A caregiver may misuse a power of attorney or otherwise steal from the victim. Both the victim and the abuser could potentially view this behaviour as not abusive, so educating at least one could be a good idea.

Media

The media sucks when it comes to people with disabilities. First is the matter of celebrities with disabilities: we are mostly non-existent (although some would say I am a celebrity). When I get a good-looking guy after my money, that's when I will consider myself a celebrity. There are no A-listers with disabilities. You see the occasional Hollywood little person. Stephen Hawking would qualify as a celebrity who has disabilities. That's about it as far as people in wheelchairs are concerned. Diversity is lacking when it comes to celebrities.

Regarding TV shows, the diversity is not much better, although the number of programmes that have characters with disabilities has doubled: from two to four. I am not one of those people who assert that every show must have characters with disabilities, but more would be better. It could be that producers see obstacles such as getting it wrong, with resulting public backlash. They need to see casting such people as normal. I suggest writing letters to the editor and producers. If producers are afraid of getting it wrong, perhaps disability organisations should offer them advice.

I have a massive problem with people without disabilities playing characters with disabilities. Some people are offended by this and compare it to casting men in women's roles: doing drag. If no actors who have a similar disability are available, that would be acceptable. Otherwise, cast an actor with a disability for a character who has a disability. Some people say you can't cast people with disabilities because every disability is different, but this argument is stupid. I recognise, of course, that impairments are different and am not saying we need to match disabilities exactly. A person with a disability could easily act out the character's symptoms. People in wheelchairs can't play able-bodied people, so if they have the required skills, let them play the roles that they are able to.

Characters with disabilities should be sex positive, in my opinion, as much as the other characters. People with disabilities are not seen as sexy. We need to challenge this. I don't consider Artie on the television show Glee to be sex positive. For example, everyone was doing a shirtless photo shoot and Artie was in cutesy outfits instead of going shirtless. I don't watch Glee and was told that this was because he was sensitive about a scar that he has. I don't particularly agree with the way it was written, but it's not my show. I don't think this does people with disabilities any good, as it signals they are fragile and not sexy. You can disagree, and say covering body image issues is important, but the producers could have done such a story line with many other characters. Media has the ability to change people's perceptions, so it would help if we could use it in a positive way. At the end of the day, I think the producers should get the final say.

News media can be mixed. You get good reporters, and some who are somewhat ignorant. In dealing with journalists recently, I always like to correct and educate when I can. For example, I told a reporter not to say I was "suffering" from cerebral palsy because people's perceptions simply won't change if the media continues to use such negative language. It is fair to say people suffer from depression. I don't suffer from cerebral palsy, I have cerebral palsy. Similarly, some people also don't like being called "wheelchair bound". They prefer being referred to as "using a wheelchair". This is not particularly important to me, but I would advise any journalist to use the latter option. My biggest problem with journalists is the angles they sometimes use. They either cover us as a pity party or because we are doing something despite the challenges we face. In my opinion this does a disservice to the disability community as it reinforces the belief that we should be pitied. Society is unlikely to change if journalists keep on covering us like this. It is essential, therefore, that we move to change the message. I note that not all journalists take this angle, but we need to correct those who do.

Employment

Employment opportunities are limited when it comes to people with disabilities. The fact is that most businesses are unwilling to hire us. But of course, we are restricted in what we can do as well. Employers may not have any experience with a person who has a disability and therefore wouldn't consider hiring them. They could be uncomfortable asking questions such as whether the toilet is accessible, etc. They could also view their business as being inaccessible and could have distorted ideas about what it would actually cost to make it accessible. Of course, if it's thousands, it may not be financially viable for them to do so. It could be worthy to build commercial buildings with a lifetime design. I also suggest that governments hire consultants to assist employers with such issues.

I disagree with the concept of sheltered work places. I think the disability community should be integrated whenever possible. I recognise that some people may feel comfortable with this, and that some people do need supervision. Sheltered work places are bad for integration and visibility. But at the end of the day, I am against telling people how to live their lives. So if they are comfortable with a sheltered work place, that's fine.

I think there are better solutions for employment. I would be concerned that these places may be open to low wages.

People with disabilities have the potential to be exploited in the work place. In New Zealand you can get a minimum wage waiver. People also report work place bullying, but this is certainly not unique to us. Wages should, of course, be fair for all, though in my opinion the majority of employees don't get fair wages. It may be worth noting that some workers with disabilities may not be as productive as other workers.

Some people with disabilities can be creative. Many turn to self-employment. Some are comedians. I am a strong advocate of regular jobs for people who encounter disabilities, such as work in offices or call centres. But this is also a new age, where you can easily work at home. Alternatives to the standard nine-to-five office job must be considered.

Personally, I like my new ventures, which consist of performing stand-up comedy and book writing. I like the creative nature of these roles. Book writing allows me to teach. I can travel with stand-up comedy. I would also be able to use my books to travel and present at conferences. It was suggested that a person who has a disability may use comedy "as a way out". A way out of what, I am wondering. I am certainly using my disability in my career, but what I do is in no way because of my disability. I am a comedian because I like making people laugh. That's extremely simple. As for books, this is only my first. I plan to write about many different topics. It is a way of educating people.

Visibility and accessibility

I believe that visibility is critical, but so is accessibility. Most things in life come down to accessibility, especially to a person like me. If a place isn't accessible, I can't go. If a computer isn't accessible, I can't use it. If no good accessible transport is available, I can't go places. Accessibility is vital.

Regarding buildings, we encourage a lifetime design, also called a universal design. This is particularly important for one-story buildings and is mostly inexpensive. Sometimes doors have lips on them; you can easily make them into ramps to make the building accessible. Bigger ramps might be more expensive and elevators even more expensive. It is more cost-effective to build these things at the beginning rather than after the structure is built. If you sell primarily offline, the lack of accessibility means a sector of the population can't do business with you, which could result in lost revenue. Also, people are living longer. Accessible design will result in more people with age-related disabilities doing business with you.

Mainstream technology varies in its level of accessibility. There is no perfect solution for Windows so I am developing my own. I found the Windows XP operating system to be better than Windows 7. Unfortunately, technology companies regularly get bought out. This can mean they stop supporting their products or their new versions are unworkable. I spent a fair few years on a Mac before anything remotely usable appeared for Windows. I can't operate most cell phones. Most video game consoles and graphical computer games are also inaccessible. This basically means I am locked out of the market, for the most part, along with my money.

A city needs to have good accessible public transport and taxis. Otherwise, people with disabilities can't go anywhere, especially at short notice. This is important for the locals and for people visiting the city. The best way appears to be using accessible cars for taxis, as they are compact and use less fuel than a van. Sydney and Los Angeles have lots of them and do a pretty good job at delivering taxis promptly. San Diego has trains with completely automated ramps. This should be the standard for this type of public transport.

It all comes down to accessibility and visibility. If society is not accessible, we cannot be visible. If we are not visible, some people are unlikely to know how to treat us. The media can help or hinder people's perceptions. Therefore, it is essential that we use it to help our cause.

Activism and politics

Regarding politics and disability groups, I think work could be done. We are underrepresented in politics, especially at the upper end of the spectrum. Any disability political group or activism organisation should move productively to create real practical change. To achieve such change it needs to work with others and form alliances. Senior groups may make good allies because many seniors have disabilities, are affected by accessibility, etc. The more people are on your side, the easier pushing for change becomes.

The problem with some disability groups is that they sometimes argue about irrelevant things, such as labels. Some prefer the phrase "people with disability" but some prefer the phrase "disabled person". The problem with this kind of discussion is that the two sides are unlikely to agree. Such discussions can be endless. While they are arguing internally, they are not sorting out things like accessibility and transportation. If a group can't do productive things, it's pretty much useless.

Political parties should have disability branches that push for productive policies and encourage their members to become representatives of the people. Encouraging candidacy could also mean encouraging people to be city councillors or serve on community boards. A party should work together with other branches and seek out potential members. It should form alliances with disability organisations, though many organisations like to be apolitical. I personally encourage cross-party cooperation when possible. But I understand that politics is heavily involved in the team mindset, instead of working across all parties. Cross-party cooperation can sometimes mean all parties agree about screwing the people. Such branches may consider getting donations from the families of people with disabilities, or mobility companies. They could also have fund raisers. Political organisations can be an effective way of pushing for change. So it is important that they find ways to get resources and be effective.

Voter turnout is generally lower when it comes to people with disabilities, particularly among the unemployed and seniors with disabilities. This is partly due to transport issues. Also, many people who have disabilities may not be aware of the differences between the parties. Any serious political party should arrange mass transport for people who experience a disability. This could be as simple as encouraging care homes to transport their residents to polling stations. Depending on the resources, a party might want to hire a few vans for the day, that is, of course, subject to the legalities and if the process is free from interference. Volunteers may also be an option. Candidates and/or volunteers may want to go into care homes or disability events like committee meetings to communicate their policies. The branch's members may want to write letters to the editor or contribute articles in a disability organisation's newsletter, encouraging people with disabilities to vote.

Different disabilities may have different issues. Braille could be a priority to people who are blind. Transport could be important to people who use wheelchairs. I do not think it is worthwhile to focus only on issues that affect everyone, such as employment. I think the best approach is to let members take charge of issues important to them and for the group to focus on issues that affect everyone. Encourage people to assist other people's causes when possible.

You don't necessarily have to be politically active to be an activist. Being independent may give you the ability to reach more people. Many disability organisations are apolitical. If you want more freedom, you could start your own organisation, do presentations or write a book. I plan to do more independent advocacy as time goes on.

Miscellaneous issues

This is my view on the label debate: your label debates are stupid and I don't care. Some people don't like the word "disabled" and prefer the term "people with disabilities". Some people find being called "disabled" disempowering. This is not my attitude at all. I couldn't give two hoots about being labelled disabled. I understand such people's argument. But I completely disagree with the argument on a personal level. The only people I disagree with more are the people who like the term "disabled" and refuse to buy into political correctness. Even though I disagree with the politically correct crowd, getting involved in endless circular debates to keep the term "disabled" is an utter waste of time. I tend just to agree with the politically correct crowd, in hopes the argument ends as quickly as possible. Take the victory and move on.

Many people don't like certain words such as "retard", "cripple" and "spastic". They don't like the first because it is a medical term. It is interesting to note that "idiot" and "moron" were also once medical terms. I don't particularly use the word "retard". The word doesn't appeal to me. Regarding "cripple" and "spastic", I have mostly trained myself so words don't affect me. I believe words only have the power we give them and that this attitude should be widespread. Such words are also used for comedic purposes. For example, I am a comedian and sometimes go by the name "Grumpy Cripple", hence this book's title. You can't seriously expect me to be affected by these things. For all I care, you can call me a spastic cripple. I understand that ignoring words is easier said than done for most people, and that is why this attitude should be taught at an early age.

Some people correct others when they say "electric chair" and not "electric wheelchair". I am amused by the corrections. Why does it matter? Nobody is going to confuse a mobility device for an actual electric chair. That's ridiculous. I know people would think electric chairs are awful and don't want to associate them with the disability community. Perhaps they are thinking too much about these things and should just chill out.

Some people want to be cured. Some don't. I would fall into the first category. I accept my disability, but if there was a cure I would surely take it. This may seem inconsistent to some people. They question if you can truly accept your disability if you want to be cured. I don't like my disability, but I can live with it. My disability is a problem, but not a big one. Perhaps you can think of it as accepting things in the moment but if you could change something, you would. I mostly can talk in my fantasies and dreams, but I am not specifically fantasising about being able to talk. I also don't fantasise about being able-bodied. I fantasise just like everyone does. These fantasies are not related to my disability. I don't think too much about it, as it is my normality. But if I could change it, I would.

Some people are completely happy with their disability and wouldn't change it. That is their perspective, and I respect that. People also get upset about society automatically assuming everyone must want to be rid of their disabilities. For my part, I think that it is a personal thing. If you want to be cured, follow that path. If not, that's also fine. While there's a section of the disability community that wants cures, many people will think this is the norm. I think to change this you need to educate people about how many people are happily living with a disability and don't view it as a bad thing. One concern is that the money spent on cures, that may never happen, would be better spent on things like technology to make people's lives easier. I think this is a completely ridiculous argument. If you want to look at money vacuums, look no further than the money paid to celebrities and athletes. I don't think enough is invested in cures, but of course I support a heavy increase in funding for technology to make life easier for people with disabilities.

I was considering treatment for cerebral palsy with stem cells. I have decided against it, for now. Such treatments are targeted at children, because the treatment has more of an effect on younger brain cells and almost none when you're an adult. I decided that if the results were going to be minimal, it was not going to be worth it. If the science gets better, I would probably give it a go. Until then, I believe the best ways to improve lives are through advocacy, teaching people and developing technology.

Communication as non-verbal

I am nonverbal. I can make sounds but cannot talk. Communication can be somewhat difficult and slow, especially in group situations. People who cannot talk usually use one of two communication methods: a communication device or pointing to things on a tray. Both have advantages and disadvantages.

I started communicating by pointing to symbols on my tray, and then moved on to letters. As far as I know this is still recommended. This method works best among people who know me because they know the way I point and can predict what I am saying. Predictions can be quicker but when someone incorrectly predicts five times before you move on to the next letter, it can be annoying. Perhaps you should predict on the second or third letter rather than the first, depending on your accuracy. It is almost impossible to communicate with people who have dyslexia. Depending on the situation you might want to write the letters down. People on the receiving end not only have to worry about spelling but also remembering the words. An additional problem in groups is that someone needs to read what the person with a disability is saying, though if only one person is speaking at a time, the group usually helps each other read.

My first communication device was something I operated through a knee-switch scanning system. I had it at school but decided it wasn't for me because it was painfully slow. When I was 23, I got an eye gaze system. People didn't think eye gaze would work with people who have cerebral palsy because of how much we move our heads. I have never been one to listen to conventional wisdom. Unfortunately, the device I had died and the model was discontinued. So I had to wait two or three years to get a new device. The new device does not handle my movements well but I can still use it, provided I am relaxed. Live conversations can sometimes be problematic. Other times I am fine. Group conversations can also be challenging: by the time you type a sentence, the group has sometimes moved on to a new topic. The current device is far from perfect, but has been an invaluable help in meetings etc.

I get asked why I don't use text language to communicate. I think the reason is that I don't use the language. My word prediction on my computer does not use it; I also use this system to send text messages, which I don't do often. I figure that, because of prediction, it's just as easy for me to type a few letters then select the word, rather than type out an abbreviated version.

As I said at the beginning, my brother has a theory about why I am so blunt. I tend to communicate my immediate thoughts; I generally don't stop and think before I say something, because it takes so long to get out what I want to say. I have never learned the art of tact. You could conclude that your communication method also has an effect on how you communicate to others, and possibly your attitude.

Sports

Mum once said to me, some people think that sport is all that people with disabilities are interested in. This is definitely not true for me. I can't stand sports. I think they are an utter waste of human resources. However, for the purposes of this section, I will leave that aside and be unbiased, for the most part. On the other hand, one of my best friends loves sports. She considers sport her religion. For me, however, when I watch rugby I am just there to get drunk, or I am checking out the players' rear ends. Either way, I couldn't give a toss about the score.

When I was younger I played boccia, which is basically indoor bowls. I couldn't throw so I rolled a ball down a tube. I was very good at it and toured all over New Zealand. Eventually I lost interest. Now I have new interests that are more creative and still allow me travel. I don't see me taking on boccia again. I also thought about taking up professional swimming but decided against the idea for various reasons. I do like the occasional swim and spa. I don't think I have the time or desire to practice as a professional. I used to swim recreationally regularly on Sundays many years ago. Now I don't really swim at all.

I strongly dislike the Paralympics, but not for the reasons you might think. I do dislike them for the standard reasons, but aside from that, I think it is absurd that we have our own version of the Olympics. Our sports should be displayed alongside regular sports and given equal screen time. I understand that it comes down to demand. On the other hand, very few people are interested in figure skating if it's not the Olympics. The commercial demand may be minimal, but at the very least we should perform at the same time as the rest of the athletes.

Interest in general is weak for disability-originated sports. This affects the sports' financial viability; they are less likely to get sponsorships from corporations or small businesses. However, charities do usually go a long way to support such sports and teams do sometimes engage in fund raising. You are unlikely to see a brand name on a player's t-shirt. This may be a good thing, depending on your perspective. If you dislike this situation I would encourage people to watch the sports, and maybe put tournaments on the internet. This could be a way to raise small amounts of money over the long term through advertisements. It could possibly be a recruiting tool for the team. You should also encourage the mainstream media to cover the events as much as possible. If national outlets won't cover them, try local stations and public broadcasting.

In general the sports community is very supportive of fans with disabilities. Athletes take pictures with them, and generally know the regulars. They could get preferential treatment such as meeting a player ahead of the rest. I remember that I went into a locker room, on invitation, well, hopefully anyway.

Someone took off their shorts, signed them and gave them to me. I think that it is a good thing that many people with disabilities get enjoyment in this way.

The final rant

This is not the end of my teachings; I have much more to say. My next book will contain information on carers, travelling, immigration, technology and a variety of other topics. It will be in the same style of humour and serious points. To find out more about me, go to www.thanepullan.com and if you want to subscribe to my memes about disability, 'like' the Grumpy Cripple page on Facebook.

About the Author

In 2014 I shifted my life focus drastically. This was the year that I started performing stand up comedy, programming accessibility software and began writing a book; this one that you're holding, in fact.

In comedy I won the 2014 South Island RAW comedy competition and appeared on Seven Sharp and the 3 News website. I did a one-hour show that year and have supported other professional comedians. I maintain a page on Facebook called "Grumpy Cripple" and release videos on YouTube.

I am programming accessibility software for commercial release. I initially needed a text-to-speech queuing system so that I could perform stand up comedy. Shortly after, I branched into accessibility software so that people like me can use computers more effectively. I am also programming word-prediction software. I hope to launch my accessibility software company in late 2015 and do innovative projects going forward.

I have previously written articles for the Cerebral Palsy Society of New Zealand and Attitude Live. This debut book is just the first taste of Teachings of a Grumpy Cripple, which is soon to expand into a multi-volume series.